THE SON WILL SHINE AGAIN

Daniel 12:3 (NLT)

Those who are wise will shine as bright as the sky, and those who lead many to righteousness will shine like the stars forever.

Copyright © 2017 by Tamara C. Denson

All rights reserved. No part of this publication may be reproduced, distributed, or transmitted in any form or by any means, including photocopying, recording, or other electronic or mechanical methods, without the prior written permission of the publisher, except in the case of brief quotations embodied in critical reviews and certain other noncommercial uses permitted by copyright law. For permission requests, write to the publisher, addressed "Attention: Permissions Coordinator," at the address below.

Simply The Truth Publishing
1310 Oak crest Drive #823
Columbia, SC. 29223
simplythetruth@yahoo.com

Ordering Information:
Quantity sales. Special discounts are available on quantity purchases by corporations, associations, and others. For details, contact the publisher at the address above.
Orders by U.S. trade bookstores and wholesalers. Please contact Big Distribution: Tel: (337) 208-7044; Fax: (803) 550-9354

Printed in the United States of America

First Edition

THE SON WILL SHINE AGAIN

Proverbs 3:5-6 New King James Version (NKJV)

⁵ Trust in the LORD with all your heart,
And lean not on your own understanding;
⁶ In all your ways acknowledge Him,
And He shall direct your paths.

Dedication

First and foremost I would like to dedicate this book to the most-high God who bless me with the gift of writing. Thank you for allowing me to use my gift to glorify you. This Children's book is dedicated to my husband Corey, son Corey Jr and Darius. I just want to say thank you for always supporting me in my writing. You all have been my greatest inspiration and I love you. I would also like to dedicate this book to my beautiful granddaughter Aubree-Rose Tamara Denson. You have been one of the greatest blessings that God has given me other than your daddy and your uncle. Grammy loves you so much. Although, God never gave me daughters he did bless me with my beautiful god daughters Myla and Sariya. I dedicate this children book to you as well. G-Ma loves you. To my God son KJ and my nephew Jacob, niece Jasmine and Jade GMA/Aunt-t loves you all. Make me proud by chasing your dreams. To all my other god children and sons and daughters from other mothers I love you all. This book is dedicate to all of you. To my mother who I take my writing after and my sister who is a silent writer in her own right. I dedicate this book to you. Love you all.
Tamara C. Denson

THE SON WILL SHINE AGAIN

John 14:13-14 New King James Version (NKJV)
13 And whatever you ask in My name, that I will do, that the Father may be glorified in the Son. 14 If you ask[a] anything in My name, I will do it.

Philippians 4:6-7 New King James Version (NKJV)
6 Be anxious for nothing, but in everything by prayer and supplication, with thanksgiving, let your requests be made known to God; 7 and the peace of God, which surpasses all understanding, will guard your hearts and minds through Christ Jesus.

Mark 11:24-25 New King James Version (NKJV)
24 Therefore I say to you, whatever things you ask when you pray, believe that you receive them, and you will have them.

THE SON WILL SHINE AGAIN

Written By Tamara Denson

Illustration by Mandy R. Tardif

The morning began like any other morning. My brother and I would get up, wash our face, and get ready for a day to play outside. Since school was out and the summer was here we didn't have to worry about going to bed early. We were allowed to play outside all day and then stay up late at night. My brother and I were so happy and we couldn't wait to get dress. My name was Corey Jr., named after my dad Big Corey; but all my friends called me Cj. My little brother Darius was my best friend. I really loved having a little brother even though he could be annoying sometimes. He always wanted to do everything I was doing and go everywhere I would go.

We sat at the table to eat our breakfast as our mom talked to our dad on the phone. My dad was deployed to Bosnia and my mom had to take care of us by herself. I was only seven at the time and my brother was five. Although, my Dad was deployed my mom made sure she took really good care of my brother and I. It was very important to her because we all were a representation of our Dad and the Denson name. If we looked a mess, people would think that he didn't take care of us, she would always say. I didn't realize how important it was to take care of myself; but I understood it much more as I got older.

Sitting at the table eating my breakfast I didn't even think to look outside to see if the sun was shining and if anybody else was outside playing already. At 10 o'clock in the morning kids were usually outside already; playing, skating, or riding their bikes.

It was almost as if the kids in my neighborhood wanted to use every minute of the day. No time to waste; had to play. Since my mom was talking on the phone and the TV was playing, I couldn't here if any of the kids were outside. So after I finished eating and asked to be excused from the table I went over to the window to see if anyone was outside. To my surprise, what did I see; *RAIN?* Nothing but rain, coming down so hard that I could barely see the cars in the parking lot. My hopes of going outside to play was gone because of the rain. I knew this would be a day that I would have to spend inside with my mom and my brother. It was a bitter sweet moment. Even though, I enjoyed playing with my brother and hanging out with my mom, my friends and I along with my brother, were going to build our clubhouse today. We had been waiting for so long to build this clubhouse. One of our friend's dad had given us the wood we needed. And my Mom had given us some old blankets and rugs that we could use to sit on in the clubhouse. However, all that would have to wait because of the rain that God decided to send on this day of all days.

My family and I were really close but all I wanted to do was go outside and play with my brother and my friends. My mom must of heard my sigh of sadness because she walked over to the window and said, "Don't worry Cj, the *Son* will shine again." My mom was a woman that loved God and she *always* took us to church. My Dad on the other hand didn't always go. If something special was happening, then he would go. He made sure we went though, because he said, "it was important to go to church and learn about how good God is." Mom always expressed the importance of having a relationship with God. She said, that we could ask or talk to God about anything. So I turned to her and said, do you think if I ask God to stop the rain, "He will?" She looked at me and said, do you trust Him? Do you believe the *Son* will shine again? Yes, I told her bodily. Then "okay" she said, and went back to the kitchen and started washing dishes. I continue to look at the rain and said a little prayer to the Lord. I asked Him to please let the sun shine again because I really wanted to go outside and play. As the day went on the rain just kept pouring. After playing with my brother and reading with my mother; seem like the day was moving by so slow.

I once again got up and went to the widow to see if the rain was lightening up, but to my surprise there was a different view. The rain had stop, but the sun was not shining. Mom, "I screamed." Mom, "I screamed again," come here please? Though I couldn't take my eyes off the view I saw outside; I could hear the footsteps of my mother coming up behind me. "What" she said, "what is going on?" Look, I said, with a tremble in my voice, look at what the rain has done. My mom stood there looking out the window. My brother Darius came over and he was looking to. We could not believe what we were seeing. For that short moment that seemed like forever we were in shock. The rain had caused a serious flood and large dumpsters were floating all over the apartment complex. Since we lived upstairs in the large apartment we didn't know that the bottom apartments were all flooded out. There were so many dumpsters floating that one had blocked the door of the apartment building and we couldn't get out.

With fear in my eyes I looked at my mom and said what are we going to do? We are stuck my brother mumbled. Trying to remain strong, my mom grabbed me and my brother and held us close. "Everything is going to be alright, she said." "Do you trust God," she asked? "Do you believe the *Son* will shine again?" I thought my mom had lost her mind because she was acting like she wasn't scared, but I knew she had to be, because there was water everywhere and dumpsters, huge dumpsters, floating around in the parking lot. "Do you trust God," she asked again. And "do you believe the *Son* will shine again?" As scared as I was, I looked at my brother and answered for the both of us. Yes, I said. I trust God and I believe the sun will shine again.

Growing up, my mom had always told us the story about how God had created the heavens and the earth. She also told us that after God created man, they eventually began to sin. So God decided to send them a Savior name Jesus. His only begotten Son. Jesus was special. He was powerful; He was a man that knew no sin, and because he loved us so much he was obedient to the will of His Father and died on the cross to save us. My mom said that Jesus died for our sins. I didn't clearly understand why he would die for us. But we must have been really special to Him too. Mom always said "Jesus is the light in a dark place. Remember, when you are in a dark place call on the name of Jesus and he will bring the light. Jesus will never let you down. He will always be by your side. He is always listening to your prayers, even when you don't think he is. When you get older, she said, you will understand just how important it is to live your life for Christ and allow Christ to live in you. Always remember, "The Son," will, shine again.

So as I stood there, I watched my mom go to her room. My brother and I went behind her because we were still very scared, however, when we got to her room she was down on the floor on her knees praying. Whenever my mom want to talk to God she would go to her room and pray. She always told us that it was important to talk to God on a daily basis, because that's how you build a personal relationship with Him. When we talk to God we are supposed to make sure we thank Him for sending His Son Jesus to die for us. And even though Jesus is in Heaven we have the Holy Spirit to comfort us and to guide our footsteps every day so that we can live an abundant life in Jesus Christ. That was a lot for a kid to remember, but because she said it all the time, it was hard to forget. So my brother and I didn't say a word. We just got down on our knees beside her room door and silently agreed with her asking God to protect us, keep us and to cause the water to subside. She thank God for always loving and blessing our family. Lastly, she thank God for protecting our Daddy and the entire military forces. Then she said Amen, and we agreed.

When she finished, we all went to the living room and she put on a movie for us to watch. We must have fallen asleep because when we woke up it was the next day. I jump up and ran to the window, "mom, I screamed once again," "yes she said, to me softly." The water is all gone and the dumpster were no longer floating. There were people working with big machines; cleaning up all the garbage and putting the dumpsters back in their place. There wasn't any kids outside because the dumpster people wanted to make sure that we were safe. However, they had big smiles on their faces as they continue to clean up the complex. I even saw a few of them trying to look towards the sun as if they knew the *Son* would shine again. I turned and look at my mom and smile and again she said, "Did you believe the *Son* will shine again." I looked out the window and then back at her and said, bodily, yes, I did believe the *Son* would shine again.

I couldn't believe all the water that had been outside was finally gone. The sun was shining and the grass was still green. We were so happy that no one was hurt. Fortunately, everyone that lived on the bottom floors were able to get out in time. All I wanted to do now, was go outside with my brother and friends so we could play and hopefully, build that clubhouse that we have been waiting patiently to build. I looked at my little brother and saw the excitement on his face as well. He could not wait, to go outside and play and just run around with our friends. Playing outside was the best part about being a kid.

Since my Mom and Dad was always telling us how important it was to go to church and pray, I decided to go in my room and say a prayer to God for allowing the *Son* to shine again. My mama would always say a family that prays together stays together and that I was my brother's keeper. Lastly, mom and dad would tell us that one day when they are gone all my brother and I would have is each other. So I wanted to make sure that I continue to be the best big brother I could be, so I took my little brother Darius and went to our room and got on our knees to pray.

Dear God,

Thank you for loving us and protecting us. Thank you for protecting my Dad on his deployment and thank you for helping my mother to take care of us while daddy is gone. God thank you for keeping the water out of our home and keeping the people safe that had water to get into their home. Lastly, God thank you for taking away the water so we could go back outside again and play with our friends. Most of all God thank you for allowing the Son to shine again.

AMENNN!!!

THE SON WILL SHINE AGAIN
By Tamara C. Denson
The Denson Family

Corey, Tamara, Corey Jr, Darius

Darius Devante

Corey Jr. (Cj)
Aubree –Rose Tamara Denson

When you trust and have faith in God that the Son will shine AGAIN!!!

1 John 3 King James Version (KJV)

3 Behold, what manner of love the Father hath bestowed upon us, that we should be called the sons of God: therefore the world knoweth us not, because it knew him not. 2 Beloved, now are we the sons of God, and it doth not yet appear what we shall be: but we know that, when he shall appear, we shall be like him; for we shall see him as he is. 3 And every man that hath this hope in him purifieth himself, even as he is pure. 4 Whosoever committeth sin transgresseth also the law: for sin is the transgression of the law. 5 And ye know that he was manifested to take away our sins; and in him is no sin. 6 Whosoever abideth in him sinneth not: whosoever sinneth hath not seen him, neither known him. 7 Little children, let no man deceive you: he that doeth righteousness is righteous, even as he is righteous.

Made in the USA
Middletown, DE
02 November 2025